A Woman's A-Z Guide to Men

- and which bits to avoid!

Claire Fost

SUMMERSDALE

Copyright © Claire Foster 1996

Summersdale Publishers
46 West Street
Chichester
West Sussex
PO19 1RP
England

ISBN 1 873475 88 8

Printed in Great Britain.

A CIP catalogue record for this book is available from the British Library.

Cover design by Annie Jackson.
Cartoons by Tom Boulting.

Introduction:

It's a minefield out there girls . . . !

So, you think you've cracked it - finally defied all odds, and found that rare thing - the decent, attractive man. But beware, all may not be what it seems! He is bound to have deep dark secrets, or revolting personal habits that make him impossible to live with/take home to mum/introduce to your most caustic friends.

You see, no matter how delightful, how charming, attentive, adoring, amusing or entertaining he may be; if he has hideous halitosis, there is no way on God's earth you could possibly give him anything other than the boot. I know it may sound terribly superficial, but let's face it girls, it's true. Coming home to roses, champagne, Hungarian violinists and adoration can go horribly wrong if you end up gasping for breath because he has the most awful smelling feet. Similarly, no matter how delightful he may look, if he opens his mouth and instead of the anticipated resonant baritone, a treble squeak emerges, it's time to go!

The burning questions are - i) what is OK, and ii) where do the boundaries between wonderful and revolting lie? It is very tricky, as some things are really borderline. I have tried to lay down some guidelines, but these things are very personal, and whilst webbed feet and crimplene trousers send me dashing for the bucket, they may well have someone else in gasping raptures.

Here then, is a handy A to Z guide of absolute no-no's. If he has / is / wears / does any of these things - *beware*, and, ideally, dump immediately!

A is for . . .

Acne - It goes without saying that fresh, oozing pustules are utterly revolting and you must never consider going near anyone so afflicted (unless you have to order a hamburger). There is, however, a strange anomaly on the complexion front. You see, old, healed acne, the pitted skin made famous by the likes of Richard Burton and Robert Redford, is deeply sexy. Call me weird, but that's the way it is.

"When you're in love, you put up with things, that when you're out of love - you cite!"

Joan Collins

Adenoids - Well actually, it's the bunging up of adenoids that is horrible. It's that irritating nasal whine, so reminiscent of small ringletted girls on stage singing *"I'm the Good Ship Lollipop!"*, which is so intolerable, no matter how delightful the poor chap in question.

Alligator shoes - I can't be too vociferous on the subject of alligator skin shoes; or crocodile, or snake for that matter. It has absolutely nothing to do with sympathy for the poor creatures, (in fact the only good croc is a dead croc in my book) but more to do with the loathsome, oily nature of everyone in possession of such an accoutrement.

Of course, the fact that the utterly repellent Jimmy Nail made an entire song about the joys of just these items, proves the point beautifully.

Anorexia - There is simply nothing worse than a skinny, concave-chested weakling - give me a Sherman tank any day. In fact, eating disorders of any description are definitely out. Why spend the entire day preparing delicious tit-bits for the love of your life, only to have him stick his fingers down his throat immediately afterwards?

"The average guy has a pathetic body, and when guys like that see me, they feel threatened!"
Martina Navratilova

Artificial limbs - I know there is some sort of bizarre sub-culture for whom prostheses are the ultimate turn-on, but for me, alas - no thanks. I suppose it is just that subliminal fear of waking up in your beloved's arms - only to find he's actually in the shower.

B is for . . .

Balaclava - with the exception of those black SAS ones with the eye holes, which send a thrill of dangerous excitement coursing through my veins . . . (enough of that!)

"Don't starve a girl of a palava,
Dangle from the wardrobe in your balaclava!"
Victoria Wood

Bald chests - I realise that this is simply a matter of taste. I know girls who go mad at the sight of a totally bald, gleaming, oiled chest, and who would run screaming if a big hairy man lumbered towards them. Personally, the thought of such smoothness makes me cringe. I much prefer acres of fur spread across well-honed pecs.

"He wore baldness like an expensive hat - as if it were out of the question for him to have hair like any other men"
Gloria Swanson on Cecil B de Mille

Bandanna - Only South American mercenaries look good in bandannas. Your average Eric from Birmingham looks - and probably is - a dullard.

"The hardest task in a girl's life, is persuading a man that his intentions are serious."

Helen Rowland

Bandy legs - I have to qualify this by saying that huge, muscly cowboys who have just got off steaming stallions are absolutely fine. The really unattractive bandiness is inextricably linked to thin, weedy, white legs, which tend to buckle under the weight of anything greater than a postage stamp.

B is for Bandanna . . .

13

"I like my men big, smart and . . . well, let's just say, I like my men!"

Elizabeth Taylor

Baseball caps - From a very early age, my mother told me never to trust a man in a baseball cap, and I have heeded her warning. I don't know what it is, they just look so stupid, and when the wearer insists on turning them backwards, it seems to have the effect of halving an already low I.Q.

"If the cap fits, it's probably out of fashion!"

B is for Baseball cap . . .

Bracelets - Why do men insist on wearing *bracelets*? Don't they realise they might as well have "I have absolutely no taste" tattooed across their forehead? They are utterly, completely repulsive, and I would never, never even speak to a man in a bracelet.

Builders' Bottom - A recognised social phenomenon, the interesting thing is that you don't have to be fat to have such an affliction, provided you borrow your beltless trousers from a fat friend.

"He had embraced the idea of the plunge neckline - and applied it to the back of his trousers! It gave him somewhere to keep his fags, and left both hands free for scratching!"

Victoria Wood

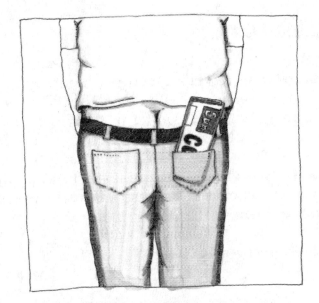

B is for Builders' bottom . . .

C is for . . .

Camouflage - Of course it goes without saying that I am not referring to MEN IN UNIFORM here, in fact, they deserve a chapter of their own entitled "irresistible". No, what I am referring to are those strange chaps who wear camouflage trousers/jackets/hats etc. out shopping, or to the pub, or anywhere other than the jungle. I usually pretend I can't see them.

"Mmmm, danger smells good."

Mae West

C is for Camouflage . . .

Cash-strapped - It's not that I'm a gold-digger, it's just that I have spent a good chunk of my life propping up remuneratively challenged chaps, and I've had enough.

"I want a man who is kind and understanding. Is that too much to ask of a millionaire?"

Zsa Zsa Gabor

Centre partings - No need to elaborate on this potential cringe-factor!

"He looks as though he had combed his hair with an egg beater, and parted it with a meat cleaver."

Hedda Hopper

Colostomy bag - I think I would have trouble sitting down to dinner with a chap who was wearing his previous meal strapped around his waist - call me narrow-minded . . .

"A man should kiss his wife's navel every day."
Cynthia Payne

Corsets - My father knew some chap who wore a corset, which creaked loudly whenever he moved. I have a bit of a problem with the vanity of someone who is prepared to wear a corset, rather than exercise a little self-control and get down the gym.

"Happiness is the sublime moment when you get out of your corsets every night."

Joyce Grenfell

Cowboy boots - I'm sorry, but they are out for any chap over 30, especially if they have spurs.

"Adolf doesn't even take his boots off, and sometimes we don't even get into bed. On the floor, he's very erotic."

Eva Braun on Hitler

D is for . . .

Dandruff - Just repulsive, and utterly avoidable in these pharmaceutically aware times.

"A weekly rinsing with bicarbonate of soda completely eliminates unsightly dandruff"
Practical Household Tips - 1926

Dead - It really helps, certainly as far as keeping a lively conversation going, if the chap concerned is not dead. It rather puts the dampeners on things, and dead people don't tend to dance very well.

"When he's late for dinner, and I know he must either be having an affair, or lying dead in the streets, I always hope he's dead!"

Roseanne Barr

Dentures - I have a friend who had his teeth knocked out playing rugby and now has falsies. For a party piece, he will take out his "plate" and hang them on the side of a glass in a pub. He can also move them around in his mouth, which is terribly disconcerting if you're trying to have a civilised conversation. It must also be rather tricky kissing someone with dentures - they might catapult down your throat at any moment.

D is for Dentures . . .

Digital watches - Especially the types with alarms on them which go off in the middle of films.

"The best bit of Ben Hur is when you see the Roman Centurion, with a Quartz watch sticking out from under his toga!"

Barry Norman

Dirty fingernails - Even worse if they happen to be long. Just imagine them running through your golden locks . . .

"I used to pick my navel until it bled!"

Woody Allen

Dyed hair - I went out with some chap for several months before I discovered the Clairol Loving Care in his bathroom cabinet. I find greying hair terribly distinguished and sexy, and the thought of him touching up his side-burns was more than flesh and blood could bare! Of course, an even more repulsive variation on this theme is streaked hair - yuk.

"I view with deep suspicion any man who actually enjoys going to the hairdresser!"

Margaret Thatcher

E is for . . .

Earring - Unquestionably out. I know they are super cool, hugely trendy etc. but you can seriously hurt your teeth on them when you nibble their ear lobes.

"I always worry about men with loads of holes through their earlobes. I never know whether to start a tapestry, or play join the dots!"

Victoria Wood

Effeminate - Just the thought of some small, smooth-skinned, perfectly manicured, scented, hairless Nancy is enough to send me dashing for the bucket. Give me a rough, hairy man with testosterone oozing out of every pore . . . Fred Flintstone, maybe?

Elasticated trousers - Especially when tailored in that funny, stretchy stuff. They are too closely associated with the statutory uniform of bus drivers to be anything other than off-putting.

"Fungus inspects his trousers, which have been marinating overnight."
Raymond Briggs - *Fungus the Bogeyman*

Expansive girth - In particular, those chaps with stomachs that are so flabby, they ooze down into their crotches and look for all the world as though they're wearing nappies.

"He's not overweight, he's just nine inches too short!"
Shelley Winters

E is for Expansive girth . . .

Eye-patch - It is really only the pink plastic variety which is unpleasant. A rugged pirate, with a worn black leather patch and a cutlass clenched between his teeth, is actually quite a nice thought.

"Love is blind . . . but watch out for the eye patch."
Cher

E is for Eye-patch . . .

F is for . . .

Fake tan - I went out with a chap, who I was fairly keen on, until one morning I saw him rubbing fake tan all over his face. A day later, it had slightly worn off, and was just caked like vile orange dye all around his eyebrows - very off-putting.

"We had a lot in common. I loved him, and he loved him!"
Shelley Winters

Fibber - So many men do it, about so many things - their income, their car, the number of children/ wives they have, their education, and of course the size of their willies. Do they think we will never find out? If they are that nice, we'll love 'em anyway, (although a huge disposable income might oil the wheels to true love a touch!).

"It's easy to make a man confess the lies he tells to himself - it's far harder to make him confess the truth!"
Geoffrey Household

Flares - No matter how fashionable they do nothing whatsoever for a man's shape. They make him look huge bottomed, vast thighed, splay footed, and as though he has a cucumber stuffed down his trousers - which most do.

Flatulence - Of course, everyone has the odd bit of gaseous seepage, but the really unpleasant types are those chaps who will ostentatiously lift up one buttock, blow off loudly, then sigh with relief. Or worse - those that try to set fire to their vile, stinking farts!

"Life's a gas . . . and so are most men!"

Ruby Wax

Frilly shirts - You know the type - those 1970's things with a huge, flamboyant frill right the way from chin to belt, usually in vibrant purples.

F is for Frilly shirts . . .

G is for . . .

Genital warts - I, fortunately, have never come face to face (as it were) with a genital wart, but the thought of them, and their proud owner makes me feel positively nauseous!

"My brain is my second favourite organ!"
                                                    Woody Allen

Geriatric - Don't get me wrong - I like older men, but when they start to become wheelchair bound, incontinent, doddery and unintelligible, they lose some of their irresistibility.

"I'm at that age, when my back goes out more than I do."
Phyllis Diller

Glass eye - As a tiny girl, I saw a film when the wearer of a glass eye took it out each night, and put it into a dish next to the bed. In the night, it continued to "look" around the room, keeping watch over its master. Nightmares ensued, and I have had a "thing" about glass eyes ever since!

Goatee beards - Men with goatee beards are either unable to grow a full "Cap'n Birdseye" affair, or they are making a social statement - either of which is distinctly off-putting. A variation on this is the full beard, with no moustache! I had the misfortune to meet the extremely unpleasant owner of a Lakeland campsite who sported this particular type of face fungus. It was clear that he has a deep psychological problem, and a flawed personality, which manifested itself in this bizarre and rather disconcerting symptom.

"I could not endure a husband with a beard on his face."
                                              Much Ado About Nothing

G is for Goatee beards . . .

Greasy hair - Especially when hanging over the collar, and plastered to the head.

Grey plastic slip-on shoes - No! It really is a question of judgement. You see, anyone who wears these hideous items must be seriously lacking in any form of reason/taste/class, quite apart from the fact that you would *never* be seen in public with anyone so attired. In fact, slip on shoes of any description other than Gucci loafers - are out!

Grubby - Unclean men are quite simply the pits. When it's good honest sweat from toiling in the fields, it's temporarily OK, but when it is old, congealed dirt, it's time to drive him through the car wash with the sunroof open.

H is for . . .

Haemorrhoids - Men always insist on talking about them, and giving a vivid description of bunches of grapes. Whilst I feel extremely sorry for victims of this unpleasant condition, I would rather they suffer in silence, particularly when I am munching grapes.

"Licking your arse must prevent haemorrhoids - that's why dogs never get them. There again, they don't sit on cold walls waiting for buses, or strain on the bog after 8 pints of lager and a vindaloo!"

Billy Connolly

Hairy back - We are talking the real fur-rug type here. The odd clump is fine, it's only when he starts to get admiring glances from the gorilla enclosure that you need to worry! I once went out with a chap whose back was just like coconut matting. Needless to say, I didn't get any further than his back!

"A woman without a man, is like a fish without a bicycle"
Gloria Steine

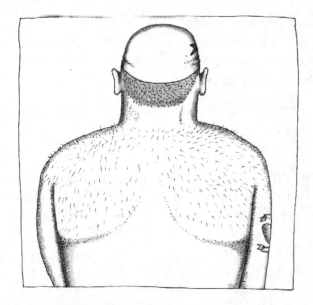

H is for Hairy back . . .

Hand-cream - Men who use hand-cream are a serious no-no. Why do they bother anyway, when every one knows a huge, rough, callused hand is utterly irresistible?

"Every woman benefits from the occasional slap around the face!"

Charlotte Rampling

Head-lice - I know that lots of small children pick them up at school, and they only like clean heads, it is just that I can't throw off the childhood conditioning that you get over head-lice, and the thought of little creatures crawling around when you're in mid-clinch makes me start to itch!

Homosexual - I have nothing against homosexuals whatsoever - I have many friends who are gloriously, flamboyantly gay. It is quite simply that they are not a good bet in the marriage / procreation stakes.

"This sort of thing may be tolerated by the French, but we are British - Thank God!"

       Field Marshall Montgomery on the Homosexuality Bill in the House of Lords

I is for . . .

Impetigo - The thought of bits of skin being shed all over the house, being crunched up by the cat, and then becoming indistinguishable from dropped Cornflakes, is quite ghastly!

"I am well aware that an addiction to silk underwear does not necessarily imply that one's feet are dirty. None the less, style, like silk, often hides eczema!"

Albert Camus

Incontinent - You may find that the constant smell of urine will overpower your Chanel, and render it useless. It is also a bit uncomfortable having to sleep on rubber sheets - especially in the summer.

"Never have anything to do with a man who is as perfumed as you "

Coco Chanel

Inflated bulge - There is a small subsection of male society which thinks that by having the most enormous "lunch box", they will be irresistible to women. They enhance what they already have by shoving pairs of socks down their trousers. The resulting vastness would terrify most of the women I know, and send them screaming away lest this monstrous weapon be wielded in their general direction.

"He (Homo Sapiens) is proud that he has the biggest brain of all primates, but attempts to conceal the fact that he also has the biggest penis!"

Desmond Morris

I is for Inflated bulge . . .

Insanity - Whilst we are all mad to varying degrees, I am really referring to people in strait-jackets, who dribble and rock all day, and have to be restrained from causing serious injury to themselves. They tend to make tedious dinner guests, as you have to cut up their food for them, and are constantly moving lighted candles out of their reach.

"Mad, bad and dangerous to know!"
said of Lord Byron

Insipid complexion - A friend of mine invited some chap back to her house for the ubiquitous coffee, on the understanding that coffee *meant* coffee! He got carried away, and started shedding his clothes, to reveal more and more glowing, iridescent white flesh, thinking he was driving her mad with desire. Eventually, she could bear it no longer, and bundled him out of the front door, never to be seen again. If he had revealed glowing olive skin, things just might have turned out differently. White, I mean *really white* skin is deeply unpleasant, especially throughout the winter, when it takes on a rather grey hue. It also shows up every blemish, and turns lobster red at the first flash of sun!

"I am very pale, owing to the drains!"

Daisy Ashford

Iron lung - It really becomes a bit of a bore getting it in and out of the car, and the owner's ability to chase you through corn fields becomes a little impaired.

"Treat your woman like you treat your plane . . . get inside her five times a day, and take her to heaven and back."
Rick Mayall - alias Lord Flash-heart

J is for . . .

Jeans with creases ironed in - Fashionable in the seventies - the height of natfness these days.

"Personally, I wonder if men and women really suit each other. Perhaps they should live next door, and just visit now and then."

Katherine Hepburn

Jeans & trainers - I have had many heated arguments about this with many friends who believe it is perfectly acceptable to wear jeans with a pair of trainers. It is not! The two are mutually exclusive. Jeans are fine, trainers are fine, but together - no! It is the male equivalent of jeans and white, teetering stilettos, and we all know how unacceptable that is!

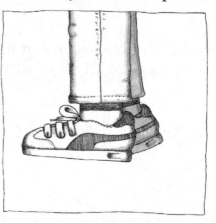

J is for Jeans and Trainers . . .

Jesus sandals - There is a great debate as to whether sandals are better with or without socks. Revolting as most men's feet tend to be, I subscribe to the "without" train of thought on the grounds that if you're going back to nature to that extent, for God's sake do it properly!

Jock-strap Of course it's fine on the pitch, but worn in every-day life is rather like a 10-year old girl with her first bra - completely unnecessary, but trying to convince the world she has enough to warrant some engineering support.

"Ah, cod-pieces. The bain of my life!"

Falstaff

Jewellery - Any jewellery, with the possible exception of a wedding ring, is utterly off-putting. Special mentions must be give to sovereign rings - especially when worn on the middle finger, and those truly ghastly thick gold necklaces that have an identity plate let into the chain upon which is engraved the wearer's - or worse, the wearer's girlfriend's - name.

"Kissing feels good, but it doesn't last as long as a diamond tiara!"

Marilyn Monroe

J is for Jewellery . . .

K is for . . .

Kipper ties - Simply not nice! Tend to come in psychedelic swirls or Liberty prints, neither of which is particularly flattering to the wearer.

K is for Kipper ties . . .

Knickerbockers - Unless you happen to be out stalking deer, any form of trousers that end anywhere except close to your ankle should not be considered to be acceptable garb!

Knitted ties - Far too reminiscent of John Osborne's kitchen sink dramas and endless wailing to conjure up anything other than anxious thoughts.

Knobbly knees - Usually white, weedy and wobbly, but always unattractive!

"I think that if a woman hasn't met the right man by the time she is 25 - she may be lucky!"

Deborah Kerr

Knotted handkerchiefs - Only a step away from Kiss-me-Quick hats and postcards of fat ladies on donkeys! As they always seem to be worn with string vests and rolled up trousers, the overall impact is very unappealing.

"I married a Kraut - every night I get dressed up like Poland, and he invades me."

Bette Midler

L is for . . .

Leather patches on elbows - These normally go hand-in-sleeve, as it were, with corduroy jackets. The exclusive wear of sociology lecturers, who tend also to have beards, BO and sandals!

"Matrimony and murder both carry a life sentence!"
John Mortimer - *Rumpole of the Bailey*

Lewd - You know, those truly ghastly people who say things like "fancy a chunk of pork sword darling?" or "come on love, you know you're gagging for it" . . . Death to all!

*"He makes you feel more danced **against**, than with."*
                                                    Jane Fonda

Lifts in shoes - Whilst short men are not top of the heap as far as eligibility is concerned, it is far better to be naturally short than to be unnaturally teetering around on four inch heels.

"Never trust a man with short legs - his brain is too near his bottom!"

Noel Coward

Limps - This is really a question of scale. Minor, gentle limps - a recent sporting injury / bullet wound is OK - in fact, quite alluring. It's when they are more pronounced and "Ministry of Silly Walks" ish , that I start to be alarmed.

"He walked with a pronounced limp. L.I.M.P. - pronounced 'limp'"

Spike Milligan

Love bites - There really is nothing more profoundly repulsive that a chap whose neck looks as though he has recently been savaged by a rabid rottweiller. Why do people give love bites? It must be rather like branding horses - to put the stamp of ownership on somebody, but I would not touch anybody who had so recently been in contact with another person's bodily fluids.

"Kissing may be the language of love - but money does the talking!"

Zsa Zsa Gabor

M is for . . .

Married - From the pure complication factor, married men are a pain. And they NEVER leave their wives!

"I can trust my husband not to fall asleep on a public platform, and he usually claps in the right places."
Margaret Thatcher

"Marrying a man is like buying something you've been admiring for a long time in a shop window. You may love it, but when you get it home, it doesn't always go with everything."

Jean Kerr

Mentally subnormal - I really don't want to spend the rest of my life doing up my husband's shoe-laces, mopping up his dribbles, or explaining patiently that his pet rabbit has died. Call me selfish, but that's me!

A man said to **Dorothy Parker** *- "I can't bear fools", to which she replied "Apparently, your mother didn't have the same problem!"*

Monk - I have nothing against monks, it is just quite simply that under no circumstances would a monk ever have anything against me.

Moustache - These fall in to a variety of categories:

1. The Hitler moustache
2. The little thin "spiv" moustache *à la* Lesley Phillips
3. The drooping "goucho" number which stretches down to the chin
4. The spectacular Victorian waxed one with twiddled ends
5. The smaller "Poirot" affair, which necessitates a hair-net for sleeping
6. The builders' large slug-like thing which covers a multitude of sins.

Moustaches are usually grown either because the wearer has no definite facial features, and wants to make up for that in some way, or because he has nasty, thin lips (never trust a man with thin lips). Either way, a moustache should ring loud warning bells for all girls!

M is for Moustache . . .

"Being kissed by a man who didn't wax his moustache was like eating an egg without salt!"
Rudyard Kipling (How did he know???)

N is for . . .

Nasal hair - I was in a meeting only the other day, with a chap whose nasal hair hung a good half inch below his nostril. I couldn't concentrate at all, and was seized with an overwhelming urge to grab hold of it and tug hard. In these days of sophisticated trimmers and gadgets, there really is no excuse for visible nasal hair (VNH).

Neuroses - The type of men who have neuroses of any kind are, frankly, not worth the effort! These bizarre manifestations of some major personality flaw and / or childhood abuse can be terrible trying, and cover a wide range of subjects. It could be only fanatical cleanliness - washing of hands, wiping of surfaces etc., or it could be something much more sinister, like a pathological loathing of gays/blacks/spiders/Bob Monkhouse/tagliatelli, or it could be something in between, such as repetitive hair flick syndrome, or *Match of the Day* addiction. Whatever it is, it is the kiss of death for any relationship - one of you will inevitably murder the other - you because you cannot tolerate him sleeping in a gas mask - or him because he catches you squeezing the toothpaste tube in the middle. Recipe for disaster.

"The days of whine and neuroses!"

Spike Milligan

Nose ring - How can I possibly elaborate on the sheer horror that this bovine accessory strikes into the heart of any girl? Any part of the anatomy which has been punctured in an unnatural and non-surgical way makes me want to vomit violently. That goes for eyebrows, nipples, belly-buttons, lips, and in particular - foreskins.

Nose rings are strictly for enormous, bellowing, salivating, swollen testicled animals, somewhere way down the food chain. Sounds like your average football supporter really.

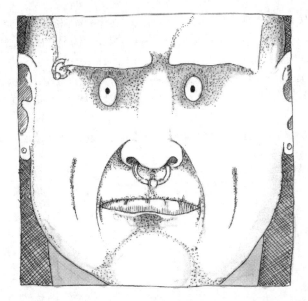

N is for Nose ring . . .

Nylon shirts - My loathing for nylon shirts is based primarily on the fact that they induce copious amounts of perspiration. This then sticks to the offending item, and causes it to adhere tightly to the flesh of the wearer, which is all rather distasteful.

"Better to have loved and lost, than to have spent your entire life with the bastard."

O is for . . .

Offal Anyone who cheerfully munches tripe, brains, pigs' trotters, intestines, ears, black pudding or anything generally designated as "not fit for human consumption" is to be given a very wide berth.

"Is it possible, that blondes also prefer gentlemen?"
Mamie van Doren

Open flies - When it is a genuine oversight, this can be excused. There is however, a rather dubious portion of society who thinks that wandering around with their flies open is a invitation to "come on down" to the girls. - WRONG! It will only outrage said girl to the extent that she will slap the offending exhibitionist smartly around the chops and march off in search of the nearest policeman.

"He was an unzipped fly caught forever in amber!"
Richard Condon

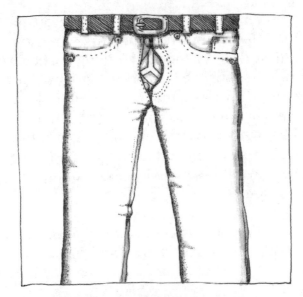

O is for Open flies . . .

Opportunist - There is nothing more off-putting than the impecunious charmer, known also as the lounge lizard. His method of working is to latch onto some nicely set-up, hard-working girl, by charming and flattering her and making her fall in love with him. He will then move into her flat, drive her car, spend her money, contribute nothing and then run off with her jewellery and her best friend. There are far too many of these vile leeches around and girls must beware.

"I would rather be an opportunist and float, than go to the bottom with my principles around my neck."
Stanley Baldwin

P is for . . .

Penile implants - The mere thought that someone could be so vain, and feel so inadequate that he dashes off and has an extra couple of links shoved in, is utterly revolting. Whilst the old adage that size isn't everything may not be quite accurate, a weenie - but useful - maggot is infinitely preferable to ten inches of de-sensitised silicone!

Plastic surgeons are always making mountains out of molehills!

Pig-tail - With the exception of Captain Bly, and Daniel Day Lewis in *Last of the Mohicans*, men with pig-tails are not to be taken seriously, especially if they happen to be in their fifth decade. What could possibly look more ridiculous than a balding, spectacled old chap, with his remaining thinning strands of hair teased and cajoled into a thin, oily, weasely looking pig-tail?

Think I'm joking? Think these don't really exist? Take a walk down Wardour St any day - the film crowd are huge fans of pig-tails, which puts them firmly in the LCT (last chance trendies) bracket. An aged, fat Marlon Brando, and a be-suited, be-sunglassed Karl Lagerfield are not any more attractive for all their notoriety.

Platform shoes - Quite apart from the fact that they make any man walk as though he has a hat stand shoved up his bottom, they are far too reminiscent of 1970's pop stars to be taken seriously, and they immediately make me want to place a thumb in each belt loop, bend forward violently, and sing "That's neat, that's neat, that's neat, that's neat, I really love your tiger feet."

"I always thought platform soles were something Alan Ladd wore to make kissing easier."

Erma Bombeck

P is for Platform shoes . . .

Poodle - As an accessory, poodles are definitely out. On the premise that a dog reflects its owners personality and characteristics, give me a fearsome alsatian, or a lithe and loyal retriever any day. The owner of a poodle - especially a pink, clipped one, is bound to be a) - gay, b) - a transvestite, c) a mummy's boy, d) - a child molester, e) all the above and to be avoided at all costs.

"Don't put all your eggs in one bastard."
Dorothy Parker

Poncho - Clint Eastwood does it beautifully - that unshaven, angry glower, and the casual flick of the poncho, whilst picking the villain off a galloping horse at 300 yards. Unfortunately for the mere mortal, it really isn't that easy, and any chap in a poncho on a wet Thursday in Cricklewood simply won't have the same effect.

Prostate problems - There really is nothing wrong with having prostate problems, except when they insist in discussing it in minute detail, or rush to the loo clutching their groin in the middle of an impassioned clinch.

"Cut the crap and show us your willy!"

Claire Foster

Q is for . . .

Quasi - Anybody who pretends to be something they clearly aren't is to be given a wide berth. You can accept someone for what they are - you would far rather know that Eustace is actually a bin-man, than believe him to be an international jewel thief, and only discover his real occupation after you've tied the knot.

"I married beneath me - every woman does."

Nancy Astor

Quick - Fingernails bitten to the . . . - Really very unattractive. Whilst a smooth, perfectly manicured hand is not the answer, a fanatical gnawer obviously has deep psychological problems - not an ideal mate.

"See what happens if you don't stop biting your nails!"
Noel Coward of the Venus de Milo

Quilted - Anything quilted, from jackets, through to waistcoats, seats of trousers and dressing gowns are a trifle dubious.

Q is for Quilted . . .

R is for . . .

Rash - Whatever the cause, a rash is off-putting. Of course, it may be something entirely harmless like a strawberry rash, but there is always the deep, niggling thought that it could be something vile and contagious that makes you go blind. Then again, would you really want to spend the rest of your life with someone who went crimson and hyperventilated at the mere thought of a strawberry?

"You look rather rash, my dear; your colours don't quite match your face!"

Nancy Astor

Rosy cheeks - Of the jolly farmer variety. A healthy glow is all important in this age of physical awareness, but *not* the village idiot look that tends to accompany vivid ruddiness.

Rubber-fetish - Really a personal view, but the thought of being trussed up like some sweaty Dunlop tyre doesn't do anything at all for me. The same goes for cling film, black plastic bags and PVC.

"Uninhibited nymph required by hard fetishist for fun, frolics, and much use of synthetic materials. Must bring own talc!"

Ad in *Sunday Times*

Rude slogans on T-shirts - Anyone who is crass enough to have vile, supposedly humorous obscenities emblazoned across his chest deserves to be torn limb from limb and fed to hungry crocodiles.

"The Japanese have perfected good manners, and have made them indistinguishable from rudeness."

Oscar Wilde

Rugby fanatic - My ex-husband was pathological about rugby - playing, watching, wearing the gear - anything that was connected with the game was sheer, unadulterated heaven for him. Saturday was always a complete write-off. The mornings were spent fielding calls from idiotic team members scrounging lifts, the afternoon was "The Match" (said in hushed tones), the early evening was spent vomiting over the bar floor, and the night was normally spent in casualty.

Sunday morning was telephonic de-brief time "what about that try then . . ." and catching up on world rugby, Sunday night was selection, Monday,

Tuesday and Thursday was training, Friday night was psyching up for the game, which left Wednesday night free, when of course, he needed to rest! Effectively, I was widowed for a large chunk of the year, and normal relations resumed from about April.

It actually wasn't that I loathed rugby, it was simply the fact that I find fanaticism to that degree very unhealthy - whatever the subject. If he had been collecting beetles, propagating geraniums or entering the world one-legged bowling championships, I would have been equally as bemused.

R is for Rugby fanatic . . .

S is for . . .

Shaved heads - Can be put into a number of categories - all to be avoided at all cost!

a) Ultra yobbish, normally worn with denim jackets with turned up collars, *Doc Martins*, and rolled up jeans, with a spider's web tattooed across the face - (*à la* Dick Emery circa 1975),
b) Belsen-esque
c) As though the individual concerned has just had a close run-in with the nit-nurse!

Shell-suits- YUK YUK, vomit copiously and reach for the bucket! How repulsive - especially when tailored in vivid, vibrant swirls of aquamarine and cerise, and in that ghastly parachute material so beloved of football supporters.

"Women created the New Man - but then they suffocated him and killed him when they found him unbearably unsexy."

Kate Edwards

Snotty noses - There are several varieties of snotty noses. There is the crusty type, with firmly glued crystals riveted to the side of the nostrils. There is the very liquid type that just drips, then worst of all is the thick, green, mucus that flows slowly like lava out of the nostril, then is sniffed loudly back in before it begins its slow descent over the lip.

"Sandy Dennis has made a career and an acting style out of a post-nasal drip"

Pauline Kerr

"It's not widely known, except by those who worked with him, that Humphrey Bogart had a habit of picking his nose!"

Diana Dors

Sock-suspenders - A la Eric Morecambe! Highly entertaining, but utterly unsexy, these are really only for retired bank managers and civil servant caught "en flagrante" with their bowler hats and brollies dangling from the bedpost!

"Ginger Rogers did everything that Fred Astaire did - she just did it backwards and in high heels."

Squint - There really is nothing more tiring than dodging up and down, side to side trying to get into line with his squint, only to discover that he is peering at some girl over the other side of the room.

"His eyes are so far apart, you need to take a taxi from one to the other."

Beatrice Campbell

Stick-on hairy chests - The real trouble with these is that they tend to come unstuck, and fall into someone's soup/the checkout girl's lap/ your mother's bowl of gardenias, which then results in terrified screams and calls to the RSPCA reporting an escaped zoo animal. They also start to peel off when the wearer dances and thus perspires copiously, and look as though a bad case of psoriasis has set in.

Bigamy is having one husband too many
- monogamy is the same.

T is for . . .

Tank tops - I was at a highly entertaining '70's party only a few weeks ago, and all my chums were done up in, flares, cow-pat wigs, medallions, green eye-shadow, denim platform shoes and kaftans. As I flung myself around in gay abandon to the strains of the Bay City Rollers, I noticed a chap standing on his own, looking bemused. I conga'd my way over to him, grabbed his lapels, and murmured encouragingly "look at you in your tank-top - you can do anything, come and dance." He replied in a

thick Brummy accent - "But I'm not in fancy dress!"
Aaaaaggggghhhhh!

"It was an enormous tank top - obviously been worn by a real tank!"
Victoria Wood

T is for Tank tops . . .

Tattoos - There are several distinct types of tattoos;

1. The "do it yourself" jobbies, where some chap has been sitting, bored, in a maths class, and scratched his name with his compass on his fore-arm, then biro-ed over it.

2. There is the LOVE HATE across the knuckles variety - normally chaps who did a couple of months inside, and tried to relieve the boredom/attain credibility by self-mutilation.

3. There is the Ann, changed into Sandra, changed into Sarah with a heart in the middle,

changed into a rather ugly mermaid clutching a banner proclaiming the words *Tracy 4 eva*.

4. There is the discreet swallow on the shoulder blade/bum.

5. There is the MAM, DAD emblazoned on the biceps, and finally, there is the eagle spanning the entire back, with lizards, serpents and strange mythical creatures encircling the torso!

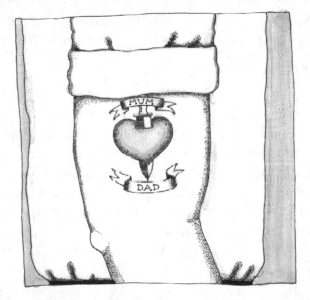

T is for Tattoos . . .

"My true friends have always given me that supreme proof of devotion - spontaneous aversion to the man I loved."

Collette

Tight T-shirts - There is something particularly unpleasant about tight T-shirts, whatever the physique of the wearer. If he is small and weedy, every dimple and concavity is emphasised. If, on the other hand, he has spent decades pumping iron, and stuffing his face with steroids, the result is even worse! Straining seams, bulging muscles oozing from under the material, prominent veins framed in white cotton - very nasty!

Tone-deaf - It really is terribly embarrassing if you are there, in church, with your hat, warbling merrily away to some rousing hymn, and all of a sudden you hear what seems to be a JCB digger close at hand. You look suspiciously around, and can't see anything mechanical. Perhaps it is an insect? Can't see one of those either, but people are beginning to turn around and look for the source of this strange buzz. Then, to your absolute horror, you realise it is your new beau, who is uttering an extraordinary low monotone growl. You nudge him angrily, and he simply turns up the volume, imagining you to be pleased.

"When people play the piano by ear, the left hand is normally completely unaware of what is going on at the upper end of the keyboard."

Trousers with crease sewn in - The exclusive domain of computer programmers and hospital porters, these are the ultimate anti-aphrodisiac, guaranteed to send you screaming for cover.

"Men's legs have a terrible life - standing alone in the dark all day."

Ken Dodd

U is for . . .

Ugly - No future! I know it's shallow and superficial to only want to marry someone who looks like a Greek god, but you have to think of the wedding photos.

"When he was born, he was so ugly, the doctor slapped the afterbirth! **Joan Rivers**

Underdeveloped biceps - Puny, thin, weedy, school-swot, twig-like arms - all utterly foul. It's not that bulging, pulsating, veined biceps à la Mr Universe are the answer - just somewhere in between please.

The meek shall inherit the earth - that's why we call them worms!"

Ruby Wax

Underpants - This is very tricky. You see, all men look silly in just their kegs, but they are unpleasant to varying degrees. The best of the bunch are those nice soft *Calvin Klein* boxers, followed closely by normal boxer shorts. Further down the line are those yukky little tight hip-hugging pants that look just like girls' knickers, then there is the posing pouch, and those awful satin-look things. Y-fronts need a category of their own, as there are many varieties - holey blue ones - relics from school, hideous brown

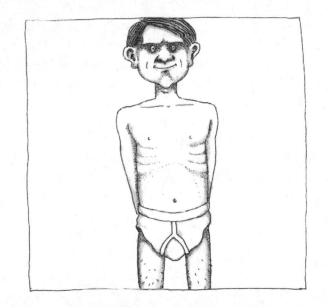

U is for Underpants . . .

and orange striped ones (come on, confess, you know exactly what I'm talking about!). The final straw are those awful tea-bag type things (1,000 perforations per square inch), which come up to the arm-pit, and hang gloomily down from the wearer's bum!

"I scramble into my clothes - whatever is on the floor, but I do put a clean pair of underpants on - by Friday, I've got 7 pairs on!"

Pamela Stephenson

Unpleasant odour - There are a variety of body odours that are unacceptable, and it very much depends on the source, as to their degree of unpleasantness. Sweat can be delightful, or make you gag violently, depending on whose sweat you inhale.

The most criminal of all odours has to be vast amounts of cheap aftershave. I had a meeting the other day with some chap who looked like a child molester with heavy-lidded eyes. That in itself was bad enough, but his vileness was compounded by the fact that he was drenched in some stomach churning concoction which sent me gasping for air.

When he had gone, the smell lingered for several days, causing wry comments from bored colleagues about the uses my office was put to.

I went out with some extremely nice chap who was renovating his house, and who always smelled of cement. To this day, I can't walk past a building site without having a little rush of adrenaline!

"I wandered, lonely as a cloud . . . because I had B.O."

V is for . . .

Vain - There are some men who are so unbelievably, nauseatingly vain, and who elbow you out of the way so they can glimpse their own image in any passing mirror. Yuk! I know a chap whose hair is so perfectly coifed, combed and set, that you can always see the comb marks in it. Infinitely preferable are the rugged, unkempt chaps who shun the hair gel in favour of the rumpled, 'I've just showered and this is how it ended up' look.

*"Men look **at** themselves in mirrors - women look **for** themselves."*

Oprah Winfrey

Venereal diseases - It may have been OK for Henry VIII to drift into a syphilitic decline, but is just not de rigeur these days!

"There's a bloody sight more pox than pax about that boyo!"

James Joyce, of Edward VII

Vertically-challenged - I am tall - about 5'10, and I have spent a good chunk of my life slumped against walls, walking with a stoop and shuffling around trying to telescope my spine. I am, quite simply, not prepared to spend the rest of my life in flat shoes walking in the gutter. If I was under 4', I would be content with a short-arse, but I want some huge, tall, dominant giant to make me feel like a fairy! There is also the problem of "small man syndrome", you know, the short gits who make up for their diminutive stature by acting like a dictator - I really can't be bothered with all that.

"Better to have loved a short man, than never to have loved a tall!"

Dorothy Parker

Vest - I know it serves a very practical purpose, but really and truly, a glimpse of a vest is not likely to send the average girl into throes of ecstasy. The best type are those t-shirty things that the Yanks wear, and the very pits are stained string vests à la Rab C. Nesbit. The fact that they are worn in summer to absorb sweat doesn't increase their appeal!

"I do not believe in the afterlife - although I will bring a change of underwear!"

Woody Allen

V is for Vest . . .

Virgin - There are several schools of thought on this one - some of my friends fantasise about corrupting a smooth-skinned schoolboy, I personally prefer the seasoned professional, who doesn't fumble too much. Having said that, my best chum and I recently spent a wet Sunday in the chapel at Eton perving at all the choir-boys, although that was more from a "potential" point of view.

"Virgin - don't be ridiculous. Everyone knows they're extinct!"

Ruby Wax

Vomit-stained - Life is too short to spend it attaching bibs to chaps who cannot control their bodily fluids.

W is for . . .

Webbed feet - I have a friend who has webbed feet, and one tipsy afternoon, I was so appalled that I chased him around a boat brandishing some scissors trying to perform a simple operation. He wasn't keen on having the webbing snipped, so I had to content myself with witty comments about *The Man from Atlantis*.

Wet handshakes - That hideous floppy hand, the clammy palms and weak, crushable fingers are enough to send me dashing for safety.

"His handshake should only be used as a tourniquet!"
Marilyn Monroe on Joe di Maggio

White eye-lashes - This really is my absolute pet hate! No matter how delightful, charming, rich and amusing he may be, if he has white eye-lashes, there can be no future.

"Robert Redford has turned alarmingly blond. He's gone past aluminium, he must be plutonium - to match his teeth!"

Joan Rivers

White socks - Not only would I never go out with anyone sporting this alarming style, but I would also never employ them!

X is for . . .

Xenophobic - Phobias of any description I find rather off-putting and puzzling, but the hatred of xenophobia, if directed towards me during a squabble, would be enough for me to pack up and head for the hills pronto.

On hearing that President Calvin Coolidge had died, **Dorothy Parker** *said "How could they tell?"*

Y is for . . .

Yellow-stained nicotine fingers - There is something fundamentally revolting about this - I know it can happen easily, but what's wrong with a weekly soak in bleach?

"When I don't smoke, I hardly feel as if I'm living. I don't feel as if I'm living unless I am killing myself!"

Russell Hoban

Yob - Football supporters, chewers of gum, wearers of *Doc Martins*, possessors of flick knives, muggers of old ladies, proud holders of criminal records, drivers of Ford Capri's, owners of pit-bulls are all non-starters.

Y is for Yob . . .

Z is for . . .

Zealot - Any fanatic is worrying, whether it be an all-consuming urge to become the holder of the world black pudding throwing record, or religious nuts who strap themselves to burning funeral pyres. It is the streak of mania - however embryonic, that is to be avoided if at all possible.

"I'm not just involved in tennis - I'm committed to it. Do you know the difference? Think of ham and eggs. The chicken is involved - the pig is committed!"

Martina Navratilova

Zero sense of humour - There is nothing more demoralising than cracking hysterical and witty jokes, only to be rewarded with a blank, uncomprehending gaze. The ability to make me roll around clutching my stomach, gasping for air and dashing to the loo to avoid certain embarrassment is absolutely essential for any successful relationship.

"I haven't laughed so much since my husband died!"

Zombie - From a purely aesthetic point of view, some chap wandering around with grubby bandages hanging off him, bolts through his neck, and the smell of rotting flesh floating around is not the sort you want to take home to mum! He will also be fairly limited in the repartee stakes, (see *Yob*, above) as his tongue will undoubtedly have been torn out by vultures!

Z is for Zombie . . .

Other Humour Books from Summersdale

How To Chat-up Women
Stewart Ferris £4.99

How To Chat-up Men
Amy Mandeville £4.99

How To Stay Married
Dick Hills £4.99

500 Chat-up Lines and Put Downs
Stewart Ferris £4.99

101 Uses for a Losing Lottery Ticket
Shovel/Nadler £3.99

101 Ways To Spend Your Lottery Millions
Jenny Humphreys £3.99

Men! Can't Live with them, Can't live with them
Tania Golightly £3.99